Ghoulicious
HALLOWEEN
TREATS

by Ruthie Van Oosbree and Tamara JM Peterson

CAPSTONE PRESS
a capstone imprint

Dabble Lab is published by Capstone Press, an imprint of Capstone.
1710 Roe Crest Drive, North Mankato, Minnesota 56003
capstonepub.com

Copyright © 2026 by Capstone. All rights reserved. No part of this publication may be reproduced in whole or in part, or stored in a retrieval system, or transmitted in any form or by any means, electronic, mechanical, photocopying, recording, or otherwise, without written permission of the publisher.

Library of Congress Cataloging-in-Publication Data is available on the Library of Congress website.
ISBN: 9798875221248 (hardcover)
ISBN: 9798875221200 (ebook PDF)

Summary: Planning a ghoulicious party? Then it's time to cook up some ghoulicious Halloween treats! Brew up a colorful batch of hot chocolate fit for a witch's cauldron. Dip strawberries in white chocolate to create ghoulish ghosts. Make a bowl of gelatin worms to freak out your friends. These fun and spooky treats will be the hit of any Halloween party!

Image Credits: iStock: yuphayao phankhamkerd, 6 (bowl); Mighty Media, Inc. (project photos); Shutterstock: Flaffy, Front Cover (left background), JeniFoto, 4-5, Maglara, Front Cover (middle background), Savanevich Viktar, Front Cover (right background), tomertu, Front Cover (bottom background)
Design Elements: Shutterstock: Ihnatovich Maryia, Katakari, LENNAMATS, MariaLev, Yevgenij_D

Editorial Credits: Editor: Jessica Rusick; Designer: Layne Halvorsen; Projects by Ruthie Van Oosbree, Tamara JM Peterson, and Layne Halvorsen

Any additional websites and resources referenced in this book are not maintained, authorized, or sponsored by Capstone. All product and company names are trademarks™ or registered® trademarks of their respective holders.

The publisher and the author shall not be liable for any damages allegedly arising from the information in this book, and they specifically disclaim any liability from the use or application of any of the contents of this book.

Printed and bound in China. 6274

Table of Contents

Ghoulicious Halloween Treats ... 4
Wiggly Worms ... 6
Creepy Cookies ... 8
Bloody Ice Cream Float ... 10
Monstrous Mishmash ... 12
Jack-o'-Veggies ... 14
Witch's Potions ... 16
Boo-tiful Berries ... 18
Bloody Good Ghost Pops ... 20
Petrifying Pizzas ... 22
Alien Slime Pops ... 24
Bat Cupcakes ... 26
Freaky Fruit Platter ... 28

GHOULICIOUS HALLOWEEN TREATS

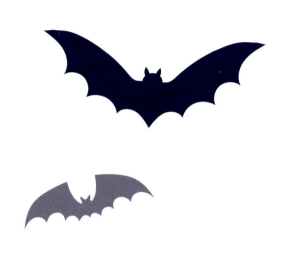

Do you feel a tingle running down your spine? The Halloween chill is in the air! Get in the spirit with a collection of **SINISTER** snacks to serve on Halloween. From **PETRIFYING** pizzas to a **FREAKY** fruit platter, the treats in this book are sure to lead to a **MONSTROUS** Halloween meal!

Spooky Supplies

Break out your baking and cooking supplies! These are some of the tools and frightening fare used in the recipes in this book.

- candy eyes
- food coloring
- knife and cutting board
- measuring cups and spoons
- microwave-safe bowls
- piping bags
- semisweet chocolate
- serving plates
- spoons
- sprinkles
- wax paper
- white chocolate

Scare Safely

Follow these ghoulish guidelines to stay safe while you prepare your Halloween goodies.

1. Ask an adult for permission before you make a recipe. Gather all the supplies and ingredients and read through the recipe carefully before cooking.

2. Ask an adult for help when using a knife or oven. Wear oven mitts when removing items from the oven or microwave.

3. Wash your hands before and after you handle food. Wash and dry fresh produce before use.

4. When you are done making food, clean your work surface and wash dirty dishes. Put all supplies and ingredients back where you found them.

WIGGLY WORMS

Serve up a bowl of jiggly gelatin worms at your Halloween party!

Materials

- disposable bendy straws
- jar
- 6-ounce (170-gram) package red gelatin dessert mix
- water
- microwave-safe measuring cup
- three ¼-ounce (7-g) packets unflavored gelatin
- mixing spoon
- bowl

1. Extend the bendy part of the straws. Place the straws bendy side down in the jar so they stick upright.

2. Prepare the red gelatin in the measuring cup according to the instructions. Before cooling it, stir in the packets of unflavored gelatin.

3. Let the gelatin mixture cool to room temperature. Carefully pour the gelatin into the straws.

4. Place the jar of straws in the refrigerator. Let the gelatin set for 8 to 12 hours.

5. Once the gelatin has set, take one straw out and run it under warm water for a few seconds. This will help loosen the worm from the straw and get any extra gelatin off the outside.

6. Over a bowl, pinch the empty end of the straw and push forward, slowly squeezing the worm out as you go.

7. Repeat steps 5 and 6 until all the worms have been emptied into the bowl.

Ghoulicious Tip

For less transparent worms, add ⅓ cup (79 milliliters) heavy cream to the gelatin dessert mix.

CREEPY COOKIES

Did one of the eyes in your sugar cookie just blink?

Materials

- premade sugar cookie dough
- 3 small bowls
- food coloring
- spoons
- measuring spoons
- baking sheet
- candy eyes

1. Preheat the oven to the temperature indicated on the cookie dough's packaging.

2. Separate the cookie dough into three bowls. Add a few drops of food coloring to each bowl. Stir or knead the color into the dough.

3. Roll the dough into 2-tablespoon (30-mL) balls with your hands.

4. Place the cookie dough balls on the baking sheet about 2 inches (5.1 centimeters) apart and bake according to the package's directions.

5. Take the cookies out of the oven and allow them to cool slightly. While they are still warm but not too hot to touch, push candy eyes into the cookies.

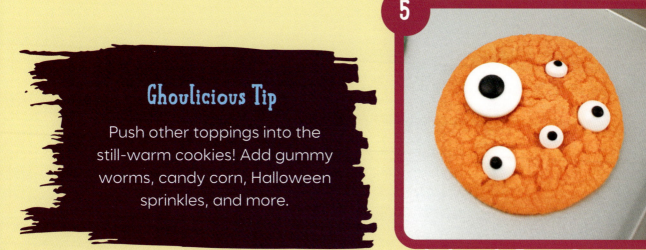

Ghoulicious Tip

Push other toppings into the still-warm cookies! Add gummy worms, candy corn, Halloween sprinkles, and more.

BLOODY ICE CREAM FLOAT

Drink a bloodcurdling concoction this Halloween!

Materials
- drinking glass
- strawberry soda
- vanilla ice cream
- ice cream scoop
- canned whipped cream
- strawberry syrup
- red sprinkles

1. Fill the glass halfway with soda.
2. Add one scoop of ice cream to the soda.
3. Spray whipped cream on top to fill the glass.
4. Drizzle strawberry syrup on top of the whipped cream.
5. Shake red sprinkles on top of the syrup and whipped cream.

Ghoulicious Tip

To add extra-scary flair, serve the float in a spooky glass.

MONSTROUS MISHMASH

Scoop up handfuls of this sweet and salty Halloween-themed trail mix.

Materials

- mini pretzels
- baking sheet
- 12 ounces (340 g) semisweet chocolate
- microwave-safe bowl
- spoon
- assorted candies, such as candy corn, Halloween sprinkles, candy-coated peanuts, and candy eyes
- serving bowl

12

1. Spread the pretzels evenly on the baking sheet.

2. Microwave the chocolate in the microwave-safe bowl for 30 seconds, then stir. Continue heating the chocolate in 15-second bursts, stirring between each one, until it is melted and smooth.

3. Drizzle the melted chocolate on the pretzels.

4. Sprinkle the candies on the chocolate before it hardens.

5. Place the baking sheet in the refrigerator for 10 minutes, or until the chocolate hardens.

6. Break the trail mix up and place it in a serving bowl.

Ghoulicious Tip

Add any kind of trail mix ingredient or candy you like! Marshmallows, nuts, dried fruit, chocolates, and more all make great Monstrous Mishmash!

JACK-O'-VEGGIES

Arrange veggies into a fun Halloween jack-o'-lantern!

Materials
- 2 dip bowls
- ranch dressing
- large serving plate
- 1 pound (16 ounces) baby carrots
- 14 whole black olives
- precut celery stalks
- knife and cutting board
- 6 baby cucumbers
- 1 yellow bell pepper

1. Fill the dip bowls with ranch. Put the bowls on the serving plate for eyes.

2. Add carrots all around the plate and eyes. Leave room for the nose in the middle.

3. Add olives to the middle for the nose. Place an olive in each dip bowl to make pupils.

4. Add celery stalks sticking up from the top middle of the plate for the stem.

5. Cut the cucumbers in half. Arrange them in a smile beneath the nose.

6. Cut the pepper into strips. Use the strips to make three lines down the jack-o'-lantern for ridges. Then use the remaining strips to outline the jack-o'-lantern.

Ghoulicious Tip

Arrange veggie trays into other Halloween shapes! Make candy corn out of cauliflower, yellow bell peppers, and baby carrots. What else could you make?

15

WITCH'S POTIONS

Cozy up with a cup of Halloween hot chocolate that looks like a colorful potion!

Materials

- toothpick
- food coloring (black and other Halloween colors)
- mini marshmallows
- 8 cups (1.9 liters) milk
- measuring cups and spoons
- microwave-safe bowl
- 12 ounces (340 g) white chocolate
- 1 teaspoon (5 mL) vanilla extract
- glasses
- whipped cream
- Halloween sprinkles
- candy eyes

1. Use a toothpick dipped in black food coloring to draw faces on several mini marshmallows.

2. Pour the milk into the microwave-safe bowl and add the white chocolate.

3. Microwave the milk and white chocolate mixture for 30 seconds, then stir. Continue heating the hot chocolate in 30-second bursts, stirring between each one, until it is warm and smooth.

4. Stir the vanilla extract into the hot chocolate.

5. Pour the hot chocolate into the glasses so they are halfway full.

6. Stir five drops of food coloring into each glass.

7. Add whipped cream into each glass on top of the hot chocolate.

8. Top the whipped cream with the marshmallows, Halloween sprinkles, or candy eyes.

Ghoulicious Tip

Instead of dividing the hot chocolate into glasses, pour it into a large food-safe cauldron with a ladle, and then add food coloring. Let guests decorate their own hot chocolates!

BOO-TIFUL BERRIES

These spooky strawberries are sure to bring fright and delight on Halloween night.

Materials

- 2 tablespoons (30 mL) milk
- measuring spoons
- 2 microwave-safe bowls
- 6 ounces (170 g) white chocolate
- spoons
- 2 baking sheets
- wax paper
- strawberries
- candy eyes
- 2 ounces (57 g) semisweet chocolate
- piping bag
- scissors
- serving plate

1. Pour the milk into a microwave-safe bowl and add the white chocolate. Microwave the mixture for 30 seconds, then stir. Continue heating the mixture in 15-second bursts, stirring between each one, until it is melted and smooth.

2. Line a baking sheet with wax paper. Dip half the strawberries in the white chocolate mixture. Quickly move them to the wax paper, leaving trails of dripped white chocolate beneath. These are the ghosts. Place the ghosts in the refrigerator to set.

3. Line a second baking sheet with wax paper. Place the remaining strawberries on the sheet. Drizzle thin lines of white chocolate over the strawberries. These are the mummies.

4. Stick candy eyes to each mummy. Place the mummies in the refrigerator to set.

5. In a microwave-safe bowl, microwave the semisweet chocolate for 30 seconds, then stir. Continue heating in 15-second bursts, stirring between each one, until the chocolate is melted and smooth.

6. Spoon the melted chocolate into the piping bag. Cut the tip off the bag. Pipe eyes and mouths onto the ghosts. Return the ghosts to the refrigerator to finish setting. Serve all the strawberries on a serving plate.

BLOODY GOOD GHOST POPS

These ghost pops turn up the fright factor with corn syrup "blood."

Materials

- 10 ounces (284 g) marshmallows
- 3 tablespoons (44 mL) butter
- 2 microwave-safe bowls
- mixing spoons
- measuring cups and spoons
- 6 cups (1.4 L) crispy rice cereal
- 9-by-13-inch (22.9-by-33-cm) pan
- nonstick cooking spray
- knife
- serving plate
- lollipop sticks
- 12 ounces (340 g) white chocolate
- 2 tablespoons (30 mL) milk
- black cookie icing
- 1 cup (237 mL) corn syrup (light or dark)
- small bowl
- red and green food coloring

1. In a microwave-safe bowl, microwave the marshmallows and butter for 1 minute and 30 seconds, then stir. Microwave the mixture for an extra 1 minute and stir until smooth.

2. Add the crispy rice cereal to the bowl from step 1 and mix well.

3. Spray the pan with cooking spray and spread the cereal mixture inside. Let the mixture cool in the refrigerator for 30 minutes.

4. Cut the mixture into rectangular treats and set them on the serving plate. Push a lollipop stick into a short end of each treat.

5. Put the white chocolate and milk in a microwave-safe bowl. Microwave the mixture for 30 seconds, then stir. Continue heating the mixture in 15-second bursts, stirring between each one, until it is melted and smooth.

6. Dip each treat in the melted white chocolate, using a spoon to cover it evenly and completely. Put the treats in the refrigerator for 15 minutes or until the white chocolate hardens.

7. Use the icing to pipe faces onto the treats.

8. Pour the corn syrup into the small bowl. Add four drops of red food coloring and one drop of green. Stir. Use a spoon to splatter the corn syrup "blood" onto the rice cereal treats!

PETRIFYING PIZZAS

These spooky pizzas make scary-good Halloween dinners!

Materials
- tortillas
- knife and cutting board
- tomato sauce
- spoon
- baking sheet
- shredded mozzarella cheese
- sliced black olives (optional)
- pepperoni (optional)
- other toppings (optional)

22

1. Preheat the oven to 400 degrees Fahrenheit (200 degrees Celsius).

2. Cut two tortillas into the same spooky shape, such as a bat, skull, or owl. Spread tomato sauce on one tortilla with the spoon. Place the other tortilla on top of the sauce.

3. Set the tortillas on the baking sheet. Spread tomato sauce on the top tortilla. Sprinkle cheese on top of the tomato sauce.

4. Use olives, pepperoni, or other toppings to decorate the pizza. Cut the toppings into shapes as needed.

5. Repeat steps 2 through 4 to make more pizzas.

6. Bake the pizzas for 15 minutes, or until the cheese is melted and golden brown at the edges.

Ghoulicious Tip

What other Halloween pizzas can you make? Try making a jack-o'-lantern, witch's hat, or ghost!

ALIEN SLIME POPS

Cover ooey, gooey marshmallows in alien slime to make an otherworldly Halloween treat!

Materials

- crème-filled rolled wafer cookies
- knife and cutting board
- 12 ounces (340 g) white chocolate
- 2 tablespoons (30 mL) milk
- measuring spoons
- microwave-safe bowl
- mixing spoons
- yellow and green food coloring
- jumbo marshmallows
- serving dish
- candy eyes

1. Cut the wafer cookies in half.

2. Put the white chocolate and milk in a microwave-safe bowl. Microwave the mixture for 30 seconds, then stir. Continue heating the mixture in 15-second bursts, stirring between each one, until it is smooth.

3. Add five drops of yellow food coloring and one drop of green to the mixture. Stir well.

4. Place the jumbo marshmallows on the serving dish.

5. Slowly pour the green chocolate over each marshmallow.

6. Firmly push the end of a wafer cookie half into each marshmallow.

7. Push candy eyes into the chocolate before it sets. Let the chocolate harden in the refrigerator for 10 to 20 minutes before serving.

Ghoulicious Tip

For the slimiest-looking aliens, move the green chocolate in a star pattern as you pour.

BAT CUPCAKES

These creepy cupcakes practically fly off their plates!

Materials

- 6 ounces (170 g) semisweet chocolate
- microwave-safe bowl
- spoons
- piping bags and tips
- scissors
- wax paper
- baking sheet
- pink and black frosting
- premade chocolate cupcakes (unfrosted)
- candy eyes

1. Microwave the chocolate in a microwave-safe bowl for 30 seconds, then stir. Continue heating the chocolate in 15-second bursts, stirring between each one, until it is melted and smooth.

2. Spoon the chocolate into a piping bag and cut off the tip.

3. Lay wax paper on the baking sheet. Pipe wings and ears onto the wax paper with the melted chocolate. Place the wings and ears in the refrigerator to set.

4. Prepare two piping bags with tips. Spoon the pink frosting into one bag and the black frosting into the other. Frost the tops of the cupcakes.

5. Gently push chocolate wings into the sides of each cupcake.

6. Add two candy eyes to each cupcake.

7. Push two chocolate ears into the top of each cupcake. Pipe noses between the eyes.

Ghoulicious Tip

Make baby bats with mini cupcakes and mini candy eyes. Pipe tiny wings, ears, and noses!

FREAKY FRUIT PLATTER

Transform everyday fruits into frightening fiends with melted chocolate and a few simple add-ons.

Materials
- kiwis
- knife and cutting board
- vegetable peeler
- 12 ounces (340 g) semisweet chocolate
- microwave-safe bowl
- mixing spoon
- piping bag
- scissors
- candy eyes
- pretzel sticks
- clementines
- celery stalk
- strawberries
- white sprinkles
- serving plate

1. Cut off one end of each kiwi. Peel the kiwis starting about one-third of the way down from the other end. These are the Frankenstein's monsters.

2. Microwave the chocolate in a microwave-safe bowl for 30 seconds, then stir. Continue heating the chocolate in 15-second bursts, stirring between each one, until it is melted and smooth.

3. Spoon the melted chocolate into the piping bag and cut off the tip.

4. Use dots of melted chocolate to attach candy eyes to the kiwis.

5. Pipe melted chocolate mouths and stitches onto each kiwi.

Ghoulicious Tip

If the chocolate begins to harden, set the piping bag in a mug of warm water with the tip outside of the water. This will soften the chocolate so you can continue piping!

Project continues on the next page.

6. Break the pretzel sticks in half. Stick one half into either side of each kiwi toward the bottom for bolts.

7. Peel the clementines. Use the melted chocolate to pipe faces on the sides. These are the jack-o'-lanterns.

8. Slice the celery stalk into small pieces for stems. Place each stem on top of a clementine jack-o'-lantern.

9. Cut the top off each strawberry and turn the strawberries upside down. These are the monsters.

10. Use the melted chocolate to pipe mouths on the strawberries. Add one dot to the top end of each strawberry to stick a candy eye to.

11. Attach a candy eye to each strawberry. Place white sprinkles in each mouth for teeth.

12. Arrange the kiwis, clementines, and strawberries on the serving plate.

Ghoulicious Tip

If needed, use the end of a toothpick to adjust the sprinkles after you put them on the chocolate.

Other Books in This Series

  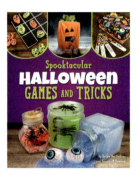 

About the Authors

Ruthie Van Oosbree

Ruthie is a writer and editor who loves making crafts. In her free time, she enjoys doing word puzzles, reading, and playing the piano. She lives with her husband, daughter, and three cats in the Twin Cities.

Tamara JM Peterson

Tamara grew up in a home that valued creativity, crafting, and reusing items. Halloween has always been the perfect holiday to create something spooky, tricky, or funny. She lives in Minnesota with her husband, two daughters, and a big orange cat.